SCIENCE DISCOVERY

Construction
Q&A

Rennay Craats

www.av2books.com

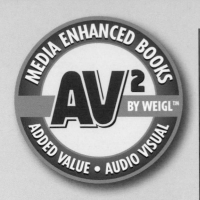

MEDIA ENHANCED BOOKS
AV²
BY WEIGL™
ADDED VALUE • AUDIO VISUAL

Go to **www.av2books.com**, and enter this book's unique code.

BOOK CODE

T 7 9 3 4 3 6

AV² by Weigl brings you media enhanced books that support active learning.

AV² provides enriched content that supplements and complements this book. Weigl's AV² books strive to create inspired learning and engage young minds in a total learning experience.

Your AV² Media Enhanced books come alive with...

Audio
Listen to sections of the book read aloud.

Key Words
Study vocabulary, and complete a matching word activity.

Video
Watch informative video clips.

Quizzes
Test your knowledge.

Embedded Weblinks
Gain additional information for research.

Slide Show
View images and captions, and prepare a presentation.

Try This!
Complete activities and hands-on experiments.

... and much, much more!

Published by AV² by Weigl
350 5th Avenue, 59th Floor
New York, NY 10118
Website: www.av2books.com   www.weigl.com

Library of Congress Cataloging-in-Publication Data
Craats, Rennay.
[Construction]
Construction Q & A / Rennay Craats.
     p. cm. -- (Science discovery)
Originally published as Construction. New York : Weigl Publishers, 2009.
Includes bibliographical references and index.
Audience: 4-6.
ISBN 978-1-62127-412-4 (hardcover : alk. paper) -- ISBN 978-1-62127-418-6 (pbk. : alk. paper)
1. Building--Juvenile literature. 2. Structural engineering--Juvenile literature. 3. Children's questions and answers. I. Title. II. Title: Construction questions & answers. III. Title: Construction questions and answers.
TH149.C728 2013
690--dc23
                         2012039656

Printed in the United States of America, in North Mankato, Minnesota
1 2 3 4 5 6 7 8 9 0 17 16 15 14 13

062013
WEP040413B

Project Coordinator Aaron Carr   Designer Mandy Christiansen

Every reasonable effort has been made to trace ownership and to obtain permission to reprint copyright material. The publishers would be pleased to have any errors or omissions brought to their attention so that they may be corrected in subsequent printings.

Photo Credits
Weigl acknowledges Getty Images as its primary image supplier for this title. Other sources: Shutterstock: pages 11, 18 and 29

Contents

What Is a Structure?

The types of structures built in a certain area usually reflect the type of land available. Where land is scarce, structures are more likely to be tall, thin buildings rather than wide, one-story homes. Skyscrapers, for example, use only a small area of land but can accommodate many people. Until the late 1800s, many structures were built by hand with simple tools. Today, construction crews use many different types of equipment and technology, including computer-generated designs, to help them build structures. The once difficult task of constructing 100-story buildings is now common practice. Builders continue to use building principles of physics and other sciences to ensure that structures are stable, durable, and safe for the people who occupy and use them.

How Scientists Use Inquiry to Answer Questions

When scientists try to answer a question, they follow the process of scientific inquiry. They begin by making observations and asking questions. Then, they propose an answer to their question. This is called a hypothesis. The hypothesis guides scientists as they research the issue. Research can involve performing experiments or reading books on the subject. When their research is finished, scientists examine their results and review their hypothesis. Often, they discover that their hypothesis was incorrect. If this happens, they revise their hypothesis and go through the process of scientific inquiry again.

Process of Scientific Inquiry

Observation

Structures come in many different sizes and shapes. Some are tall and thin, while others are short and wide. Why are structures built in different ways? What is the purpose of structures?

Have You Answered the Question?

The cycle of scientific inquiry never ends. Engineers and architects continue to improve and make better structures. They ask more questions, research new ways, and do more experiments.

Research

Engineers and **architects** research different ways to construct buildings. They look for different ways to improve buildings, making structures better and for different purposes.

Results

Construction is complex. It involves technology, engineering, and following certain principles, or rules, of physics and other sciences. Once complete, the builders may find that their design has problems. This leads to more hypotheses and experiments.

Hypothesis

Engineers and architects hypothesize that the best structures are the ones where the design fits the purpose of the structure. Structures are planned and built with a purpose in mind.

Experiment

Engineers and architects experiment with different ways of building. They design structures around their function.

What Are Some of the First Structures?

People have been designing unique structures for thousands of years. Among the best examples of early designs are the pyramids of Egypt. Some of these incredible structures have been standing for more than 4,500 years.

The pyramids served as tombs for ancient Egyptian **pharaohs**. Their construction was a remarkable accomplishment, considering that the structures were so large and the builders did not have modern machines and equipment.

Historians estimate that it took between 20,000 and 30,000 people about 30 years to build the Great Pyramid at Giza, near Cairo, Egypt. Each side of the base spans 755 feet (230 meters), and the Great Pyramid towers 479 feet (146 m) high. To complete the structure, more than two million blocks of stone were assembled.

The limestone for the base and the outside part of the pyramid came from the Nile River. Copper was brought from eastern Egypt, granite was hauled from southern Egypt, and cedar was shipped across the Mediterranean Sea from Lebanon.

❯ Some Egyptian pyramids were part of a complex that included several smaller pyramids.

Nobody knows for sure, but the ancient Egyptians may have used huge rollers to carry the blocks to the site, levers to lift them, and ramps to move the blocks to the top of the pyramid. Today, builders have much different ways to plan and construct buildings.

Digging Deeper

Your Challenge!

Building such structures as the ancient pyramids of Egypt was not an easy job. The ancient Egyptians did not have the tools and machines we have today. They probably used basic tools and simple machines, such as ramps. To dig deeper:

Research other ancient structures and find out how they were built. Make a list of the tools and methods they used.

Summary

The pyramids of Egypt are an example of some amazing early structures. In fact, the pyramids of Egypt are considered a wonder of the world.

Further Inquiry

Though they were built long ago, the Egyptian pyramids still stand today. Maybe we should ask,

When should old buildings be protected?

When Should Old Buildings Be Protected?

Around the world, people celebrate their history and try to preserve its physical remains. In the United States, people establish museums in pioneer homes to show how their ancestors lived and worked. People also tour homes that were built in the 1800s and early 1900s to experience what life was like in the past.

The historical buildings in many places are protected by organizations and governments. These groups want to see that historical buildings stay intact. Often, groups restore historical buildings so they look just as they did when they were first built. Sometimes, people do not consider the historical value of a building until there is a threat to tear it down. Then, groups rally to save a building that is important to an area's heritage.

Some people believe older buildings are not important and should be torn down. They feel that old buildings need to be demolished, often because they are run-down and barely standing. By removing these buildings, some developers argue, new life and prosperity can be brought to an area.

❯ Monticello, Thomas Jefferson's plantation home in Virginia, is considered a historical landmark.

Digging Deeper

Your Challenge!

Take a stand. Do research to find an important old building in your area that is in danger of being torn down. Write a report about the building's history. State whether you think the building should be saved, and why or why not.

Summary

Old versus new is the debate. Some people want to preserve, or keep, historically important structures. Other people want to replace such buildings with new and improved structures.

Further Inquiry

Sometimes, it is impossible to save an old building. Some old structures must be torn down because they are unsafe. Removing a building is not easy. Maybe we should ask,

How are old buildings cleared for new structures?

Q&A

How Are Old Buildings Cleared for New Structures?

Construction crews often have to demolish old buildings to make room for new ones. Small buildings, such as houses, can be leveled with wrecking balls and bulldozers. **Demolition** crews are brought in when large buildings, such as skyscrapers, must be removed from a building site. Demolition crews use explosives to safely bring down large buildings.

Demolition experts, often called blasters, use plans of the building to map the placement of powerful explosives inside it. They visit the building many times to study how it was built and how they can safely collapse it. Many blasters create **three-dimensional** computer models of the building to simulate their plans. Once the blasters are sure of their plan, they prepare to demolish the building. The key to a successful demolition is to control how the building falls once the explosives have been detonated.

Many times, old buildings are surrounded by new ones, so demolition crews need to make sure they collapse the building into itself. This is called imploding, and it is challenging work. There are only a few companies in the world that can do it.

❯ To demolish a tall building, blasters usually place explosives on several different floors.

Digging Deeper

Your Challenge!

Visit your local museum or library, or use the internet, to find photos of your city from the last 50 to 100 years. Create a visual timeline by putting the photos in order by date. How have the buildings changed?

Summary

Making way for new structures is not an easy task. For some structures, a wrecking ball or bulldozer will work. Larger structures need to be demolished using explosives, which can be dangerous.

Further Inquiry

After old buildings have been demolished, new structures can be built in their place. Maybe we should ask,

How do builders plan a structure?

How Do Builders Plan a Structure?

Contractors, builders, and engineers on a construction site rely on plans called blueprints. A blueprint is a drawing that shows where interior walls, doors, windows, electrical wiring, and plumbing will be on a building.

Blueprints are usually large sheets of paper with blue lines outlining the design. Blueprints provide exact information to the builder. This information includes the engineering and safety requirements, measurements, and a list of the building materials that are needed for the project.

A building cannot be built without blueprints. Construction workers follow the detailed plan on the blueprint to build exactly what the architect imagined for a structure. A scale is a part of every blueprint. It shows the builders the sizes of all of the building's parts and the distances between them.

❭ Very few architects still draw blueprints by hand.

❮ Today, most architects use computer programs, such as Computer-Aided Design (CAD), to create their designs.

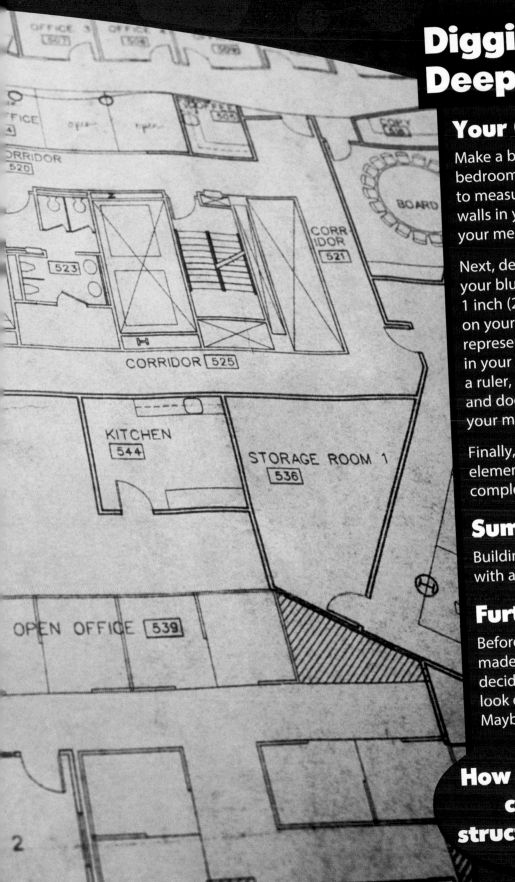

Digging Deeper

Your Challenge!

Make a blueprint of your bedroom. Use a tape measure to measure the length of the walls in your room. Record your measurements.

Next, decide on a scale for your blueprint. For example, 1 inch (2.5 centimeters) on your blueprint could represent 1 foot (0.3 m) in your bedroom. Using a ruler, draw the walls and door according to your measurements.

Finally, map out other elements of your room to complete your blueprint.

Summary

Building a structure starts with a plan.

Further Inquiry

Before building plans are made, architects must decide on the overall look of the building. Maybe we should ask,

How do builders choose a structure's style?

How Do Builders Choose a Structure's Style?

Building styles that work well and are popular are often recycled. Buildings in a particular location that were constructed during the same time period tend to share certain architectural qualities. Many factors contribute to style, from local materials, to the function the structure will serve, to the owners' individual tastes.

During the 17th and 18th centuries, American architects often borrowed styles from European architects. Among those borrowed styles were brick homes that had two identical halves. Other European styles were reflected in the **plantation** homes of the American South. These were enormous structures with simple fronts, open spaces, and large columns on either side of the doorway.

❯ Architects combine materials such as concrete, steel, and glass in unique ways to create new designs.

American architects have added their own touches to borrowed building styles. These have included shingles, or roof tiles, on country houses and metal frames for tall structures that would eventually be the basis of skyscrapers. Through the years, many styles have come back in fashion. While these buildings sometimes look the same as older structures, modern machines have been used to build them. For example, builders often design homes that include elements of Roman or Greek architecture, such as columns. Designers continue to combine styles from centuries ago with the newest design ideas to create American architecture.

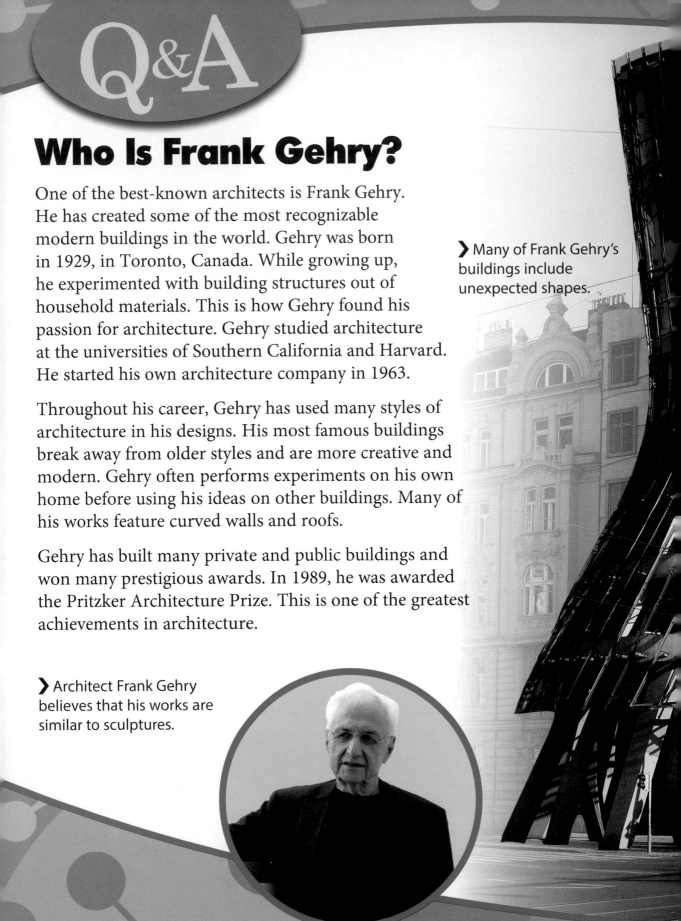

Q&A

Who Is Frank Gehry?

One of the best-known architects is Frank Gehry. He has created some of the most recognizable modern buildings in the world. Gehry was born in 1929, in Toronto, Canada. While growing up, he experimented with building structures out of household materials. This is how Gehry found his passion for architecture. Gehry studied architecture at the universities of Southern California and Harvard. He started his own architecture company in 1963.

❯ Many of Frank Gehry's buildings include unexpected shapes.

Throughout his career, Gehry has used many styles of architecture in his designs. His most famous buildings break away from older styles and are more creative and modern. Gehry often performs experiments on his own home before using his ideas on other buildings. Many of his works feature curved walls and roofs.

Gehry has built many private and public buildings and won many prestigious awards. In 1989, he was awarded the Pritzker Architecture Prize. This is one of the greatest achievements in architecture.

❯ Architect Frank Gehry believes that his works are similar to sculptures.

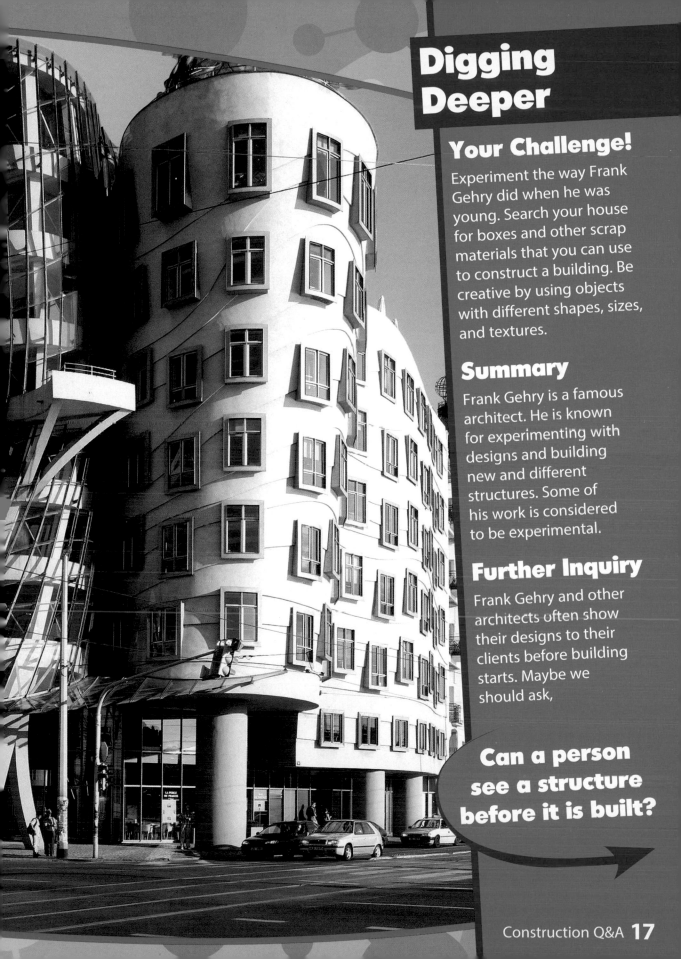

Digging Deeper

Your Challenge!

Experiment the way Frank Gehry did when he was young. Search your house for boxes and other scrap materials that you can use to construct a building. Be creative by using objects with different shapes, sizes, and textures.

Summary

Frank Gehry is a famous architect. He is known for experimenting with designs and building new and different structures. Some of his work is considered to be experimental.

Further Inquiry

Frank Gehry and other architects often show their designs to their clients before building starts. Maybe we should ask,

Can a person see a structure before it is built?

Can a Person See a Structure Before It Is Built?

It might be hard to imagine, but people can see and experience a building before it even exists. Construction companies and architects can use computer software to take clients, or customers, on a **virtual tour** of proposed buildings. The pictures created by the computer appear three-dimensional and may even include furniture and people. In such a tour, people can see a room from every angle.

If construction of the structure has already started, virtual tours can be even more detailed. In this case, photos of every room are loaded to a computer. Then, they are combined to create one large photograph of the entire space.

Another benefit of virtual tours is that clients do not even have to visit the construction site to see the building. Construction companies or architectural firms can post their "tours" on the Internet. The virtual tour can then be downloaded to a laptop, tablet, or smartphone. When clients are ready to check on a project, they can do so right where they are.

❯ Some virtual tours only show the inside of the building, but others include a full virtual model of the structure.

▼ Sometimes, architects create small, physical models of new building projects to show to their clients.

Your Challenge!

There are many free computer programs on the Internet for designing buildings. Have an adult help you search for one that you can use at home or on a school computer. You can create different kinds of buildings and even entire cities.

Summary

Technology helps in providing important information when construction projects are underway. Virtual tours are an easy way to see something without having to be physically in the same location.

Further Inquiry

Once a plan is made, the land must be prepared for building. Maybe we should ask,

How is land prepared for building?

How Is Land Prepared for Building?

There is one main challenge to building a structure—how to prepare land for building. Bulldozers and hydraulic excavators are two machines commonly used for clearing land.

The land on which a building will be constructed must be flat. To help do this, bulldozers clear dirt and rocks away from the area. They also remove large obstacles, such as trees, before construction. Once the building site has been made level, excavators use their large shovels to dig a hole for the structure's foundation. For large buildings, such as skyscrapers, the hole dug by the shovels may then be filled with concrete. This creates a firm foundation, or base, for the rest of the building.

How deep the foundation is depends on how large the building will be and how soft or hard the ground is. Tall, heavy structures like skyscrapers and bridges need a deep foundation to prevent them from sinking. If the ground surface is soft, the foundation might need to be very deep. If the ground is mostly hard rock, the foundation can be shallower.

In some areas, construction crews hammer concrete or steel columns into the ground to hold the weight of a skyscraper. These are called piles and are usually used when the ground is soft.

❯ Large excavators can dig and lift tons of tons of rocks, dirt, and other heavy materials.

Digging Deeper

Your Challenge!

Ask an adult to take you to a construction site near your home. From a safe distance, draw each type of machine you see. When you get home, research online to find the name and purpose of each type of machine.

Summary

Land must be cleared and prepared before construction can begin. Heavy machines, such as bulldozers and excavators, are important because they can do this difficult job quickly and safely.

Further Inquiry

After the land has been cleared, different kinds of materials are brought to the construction site. Maybe we should ask,

What are some different building materials?

What Are Some Different Building Materials?

Concrete was invented more than two thousand years ago by the Romans. They used concrete to build arches, domes, and roads. Although the words "cement" and "concrete" are often used to describe the same substance, they are not the same thing. Cement is a gray powder. It is one of the ingredients used to make concrete. Concrete is a hard building material that is made by mixing cement, sand, small stones, and water.

In 1824, a British inventor named Joseph Aspdin invented a special kind of cement called Portland cement. Today, it is the key ingredient used in most types of concrete because it works like glue. It holds all the parts of concrete together. It makes concrete much stronger and more versatile than earlier forms of concrete.

Today, concrete made from Portland cement is used to make dams, bridges, buildings, and pavement. To make Portland cement, materials such as clay, limestone, and sand are crushed together and poured into a large oven called a kiln. The materials inside the kiln reach temperatures between 2,700° and 3,000° Fahrenheit (1,480° and 1,650° Celsius). This incredible heat causes the ingredients to break down and form into new substances. After the material is removed from the kiln, it is cooled, bagged, and then sold as Portland cement. The cement is mixed with water, small stones, and sand to produce concrete. Once poured, the surface of the concrete is kept damp so that it can cure, or harden. The longer the concrete is allowed to cure, the stronger it will be.

> Concrete is often brought to the construction site in a special truck that has a rotating barrel. The barrel moves constantly to keep the wet concrete from hardening before it can be used.

Digging Deeper

Your Challenge!

Concrete and cement are used in buildings and for other projects. You can try making a garden stepping stone using a kit from a craft or hardware store. Ask an adult to help you mix the cement and complete the project.

Summary

Concrete and cement are not the same. Portland cement was invented by Joseph Aspdin. It allows different types of structures to be made. Portland cement is much stronger than concrete.

Further Inquiry

Cement and other construction materials are heavy. Machines move these things around the construction site using hydraulics. Maybe we should ask,

How do hydraulic machines work?

How Do Hydraulic Machines Work?

Bulldozers, forklifts, cranes, excavators, and backhoes are common machines on a construction site. These machines all operate on the principles of hydraulics. This enables the machines to do heavy lifting and pushing.

In a hydraulic system, two pistons fit into two cylinders, or tubes. The cylinders are filled with a liquid, such as oil. The pistons are connected by a pipe, which is also filled with oil. When pressure is applied to one piston, the force is transferred to the second piston through the oil in the pipe. When one piston is pushed down, the other is lifted by the oil. This back-and-forth movement powers the machine. Hydraulic systems in any machine work the same way.

Hydraulics can be used for much more than construction. Everyday devices, such as car brakes, use hydraulics. More scientific uses for hydraulics include launching systems for deep sea exploration. The wreckage of the *Titanic* was found using a hydraulic-powered submarine.

▼ Hydraulic systems allow bulldozers to push about as much as they weigh. A 5-ton (4.5-tonne) bulldozer can move about 5 tons (4.5 tonnes) of rocks, dirt, and other materials.

Digging Deeper

Your Challenge!

Hydraulic systems allow machines to do heavy work. You can learn the basics of hydraulics by building a simple hydraulic system from common materials, such as Popsicle sticks and plastic tubing. Find an easy hydraulic machine project online and follow the steps.

Summary

Machines make work easier to do, especially when building new structures. Most large machines use hydraulics. Hydraulics transfer force using a liquid and a set of cylinders and pistons. This allows machines to exert pressure to do work.

Further Inquiry

Some machines that are used in construction do not use hydraulics. Maybe we should ask,

How do simple machines help build structures?

How Do Simple Machines Help Build Structures?

Not all machines on a construction site tower over the people operating them. **Simple machines** are important in construction. These machines make tasks easier because they use only one movement to do a job.

A lever is a simple machine. It has a stiff bar and a fulcrum. The fulcrum is the point on the bar where the bar turns. An example of one type of lever is a seesaw. The fulcrum is in the center of this lever. When one end of the lever is pushed down, the other end goes up. A pry bar is a lever used on construction sites.

A screw is another type of simple machine. Screws often are used on buildings to fasten objects together. The wedge is another kind of simple machine. The jagged blade of a saw is made of many wedges. These wedges make it easier to cut through materials such as wood. A nail is also a wedge. Using the hammer as a lever, the sharp end of the nail, or wedge, can be driven into wood.

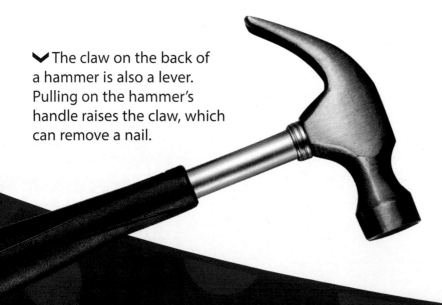

⌄The claw on the back of a hammer is also a lever. Pulling on the hammer's handle raises the claw, which can remove a nail.

Digging Deeper

Your Challenge!

There are six simple machines. Use the Internet to learn about them. Then, search your house to find as many simple machines as you can. A door hinge, for example, is a type of simple machine. Create a chart listing the name of each machine and how it is used.

Summary

Simple machines are commonly used in construction. They are used in many tools that help workers pull, raise, cut, attach, and increase or change the direction of force so work can be done.

Further Inquiry

Simple tools make work easier to do. Cranes use simple machine principles to lift heavy weights. Maybe we should ask,

How do cranes lift so much weight?

⌃ Levers were used by the ancient Greeks and are still used today.

How Do Cranes Lift so Much Weight?

Cranes are easy to spot on a construction site. They are the machines with long mechanical arms that reach high into the air. Cranes are used to hoist concrete, steel, large tools, and any other building materials that need to be moved from one place to another.

To secure a very large crane, such as a tower crane, a pad of thick concrete is sometimes poured on the ground. The base of the tower crane is anchored deep into this pad. The tower, or mast, of the crane is connected to the base. This mast supports the rest of the crane. Once the crane is secured, it is ready to lift and move materials and tools.

The operator sits in a cab. The cab is where the operator controls the crane, using foot pedals and levers to raise and move building materials and uses a combination of foot pedals and levers to control the crane and lift heavy loads. The motor and gears of the crane, called the slewing unit, are attached to the top of the mast. This allows the crane to swivel and turn. The slewing unit includes the jib, or arm, and a trolley. The jib is the part of the crane that supports the load. The trolley carries the load along the jib. A machinery arm is part of the slewing unit. The machinery arm contains the crane's electronic components and motors.

❯ There are many different types of cranes. Crawler cranes are mounted on tracks, which allow them to move around a building site.

Digging Deeper

Your Challenge!

Cranes make lifting heavy objects easier. For this activity, try to build your own small crane using Popsicle sticks or toothpicks. There are many websites that you can use to help you design and build your crane. Test to see how much weight your crane can lift.

Summary

Cranes are important machines in construction. Cranes easily move material from one place to another and up and down a structure while it is being built. Cranes can lift a great deal of weight.

Further Inquiry

Cranes help builders to construct tall structures, including skyscrapers. Maybe we should ask,

How are skyscrapers built?

How Are Skyscrapers Built?

Skyscrapers have come to define big city skylines. Over the years, skyscrapers have gotten taller and taller. As technology changes, some experts believe skyscrapers will grow even higher.

Skyscrapers grew out of the need to create the most business or living space on the smallest area of land. The challenge for early architects was to support all of the weight stacked upon the base of the building. As each new story was added, the pressure on every point below it became greater. This pressure is similar to stacking books on a person's head—the head, neck, and spine can only take so much weight.

As buildings became taller, the walls of the lower floors, which had to support the weight of the floors above them, became so thick that the rooms were no longer useable. It was possible to construct buildings only about 10 stories high using this method.

Taller structures became possible with the development of new building designs and mass-produced steel and iron. In the mid-1800s, construction companies started using long, solid beams of iron that were fairly light and easier to build with than concrete alone. A few decades later, they turned to steel, which is lighter and stronger than iron. These new materials combined with new building techniques allowed taller skyscrapers to be built. Today, skyscrapers are supported by steel beams, not thick walls.

> Many of the world's tallest skyscrapers were built in the last two decades.

Digging Deeper

Your Challenge!

Use the Internet or books from the library to research the world's tallest skyscrapers. Pick your favorite skyscraper and research how it was built. How long did it take? How much steel was used? How many people worked on it? How is the building used now?

Summary

To build tall structures, advancements in building materials were needed. Steel and iron beams allow engineers to build skyscrapers because such materials can support the weight.

Further Inquiry

People need to be able to move up and down the many floors of a skyscraper. Maybe we should ask,

How do elevators work?

How Do Elevators Work?

In some form or another, elevators have been in use since as early as 300 BC. The earliest elevators were operated by people or animals pulling ropes. The first version of the elevator as we know it today traveled only between a few floors. The first electrically powered elevator in the United States was in New York City. It was used to lift objects between different floors. Safety devices were installed to prevent the car from dropping if the rope that lifted the elevator broke. This design change made it possible for elevators to carry people. The first passenger elevator was soon operating in a New York City store.

Today, modern elevators carry thousands of pounds of freight and passengers up hundreds of floors, thousands of times each day. Without elevators, tall buildings would be very difficult to use. Few people would walk up to the 99th floor.

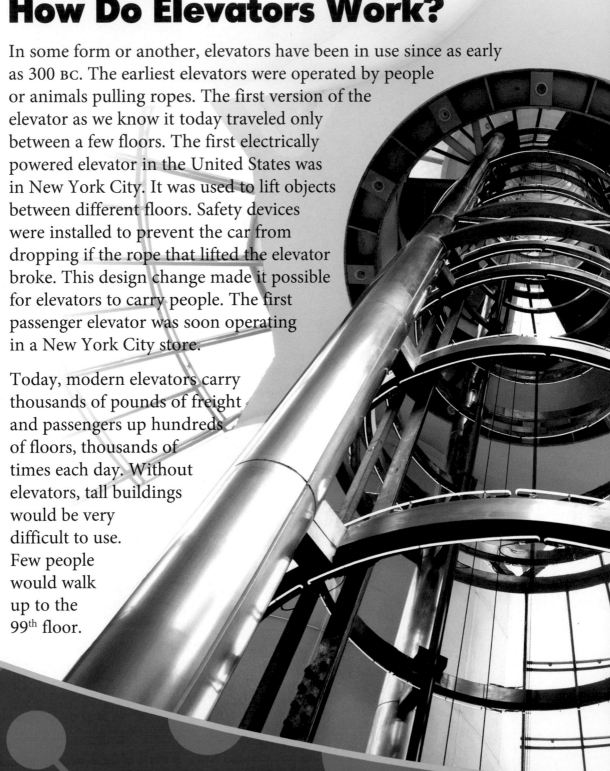

Elevators are also an important safety feature in tall buildings. They carry firefighters and other responders quickly to a floor to respond to emergencies.

As buildings have become taller, engineers have had to design faster elevators to shorten the time it takes to go up. The Taipei 101 tower in Taiwan has elevators that climb at a speed of 3,314 feet (1,010 m) per minute. That is more than three times faster than a passenger jet climbs after taking off.

❰ Thanks to new technology, elevators can be built bigger than ever before. Some high-capacity elevators can carry up to 80 people at a time.

Your Challenge!

Visit a library or use the Internet to find out how long it takes the elevator in several different skyscrapers to climb to the top floor or observation deck. Make a chart of your findings. Which elevator is the fastest?

Summary

Forms of elevators have been in existence for a long time. Today, elevators make living and working in tall buildings possible. Without elevators, it would be hard to live or work on the top floors of a tall skyscraper.

Further Inquiry

Elevators help people travel and work inside tall buildings. Maybe we should ask,

What are some of the tallest buildings in the world?

What Are Some of Tallest Buildings in the World?

Skyscrapers are a common sight in cities. Wherever land is expensive, especially in large cities and other urban centers, you will find skyscrapers. Such buildings seem to reach for the sky, or scrape it. That is where the name "skyscraper" comes from. This was not always the case. In fact, people were once skeptical that buildings with multiple stories, such as skyscrapers, could be built. The first skyscraper was the Home Insurance Building. It was built in 1884 in Chicago, Illinois. It was only 10 stories high, but at the time, it was an amazing feat to construct such a structure.

Today, the One World Trade Center in New York is the tallest building in the United States. It is not, however, the tallest in the world. In fact, only two of the top 10 tallest buildings in the world are found in the United States.

9

Willis Tower
Chicago, Illinois
108 Floors
1,451 feet (442 m) tall
completed 1974

3

One World Trade Center
New York, New York
1,776 feet (541 m) tall

NORTH AMERICA

ATLANTIC OCEAN

SOUTH AMERICA

PACIFIC OCEAN

2

Makkah Clock Royal Tower (Abraj Al Bait)
Makkah, Saudi Arabia
95 Floors
1,972 feet (601 m) tall
completed 2012

4
Taipei 101
Taipei, Taiwan
101 Floors
1,671 feet (509 m) tall
completed 2004

5
Shanghai World Financial Center
Shanghai, China
1,614 feet (492 m) tall

8
Zifeng Tower
Nanjing, China
1,476 feet (450 m) tall

ARCTIC OCEAN

ASIA

10
KK100
Shenzhen, China
1,449 ft. (442 m) tall

EUROPE

6
International Commerce Center
Hong Kong, China
1,588 feet (475 m) tall

AFRICA

7
Tower 1 & Tower 2 Petronas Towers
Kuala Lumpur, Malaysia
1,482 feet (451.7 m) tall

AUSTRALIA

1
Burj Khalifa
Dubai, United Arab Emirates
163 Floors
2,717 feet (828 m) tall
completed 2010

Digging Deeper

Your Challenge!

Use graph paper and draw the 10 tallest buildings. Each square on the graph paper can be 100 feet (30 m). Add other tall buildings to see how they compare. For example, you can add the Empire State building.

Summary

Skyscrapers were once only part of an architect's dreams. Today, skyscrapers are commonplace.

Further Inquiry

Building taller and better buildings is not easy. They must be strong enough to withstand bad weather and other natural forces. Maybe we should ask,

How do skyscrapers withstand forces?

How Do Skyscrapers Withstand Forces?

Skyscrapers can be hundreds, even thousands, of feet tall. The weight of these buildings is incredible. To help bear all this weight, architects design skyscrapers differently than they do smaller buildings. The base of a skyscraper is often much wider than the building itself. Also, the foundation is much deeper than other types of buildings. A deep and wide base helps spread out the weight of the building. Within the building itself, each floor is attached to columns separately. This means that each floor is only supporting itself and not the floors above it.

How to best support a structure's weight is only one of many issues of concern for engineers. There are also outside forces, such as earthquakes and wind. Wind can be very powerful at great heights. If a strong wind blows, a skyscraper can sway from side to side like a tree. While this movement may not damage the structure, it can make the occupants of the building uneasy. Engineers have designed a way to lessen the effects of such forces. When a skyscraper is being constructed, crews tighten the points at which the vertical columns meet the horizontal beams in the frame. The building will then move as one solid object.

> ❯ In Japan and other countries where earthquakes are common, skyscrapers are designed to sway but not break as the ground shakes.

Digging Deeper

Your Challenge!

Build a model skyscraper with cardboard boxes of different sizes. Place the widest box on the ground. This will be the base of your skyscraper. Stack the smaller boxes on top of the base. Tape the boxes together. Push lightly on the top of your skyscraper. Does it fall over? How can you make your structure stronger and more stable?

Summary

Skyscrapers are tall structures that have to deal with many different forces. Engineers have designed some solutions to build taller skyscrapers.

Further Inquiry

Skyscrapers are designed carefully to avoid being damaged in severe weather. Maybe we should ask,

How do buildings keep people safe?

How Do Buildings Keep People Safe?

Engineers are developing ways to reduce the damage done to buildings by earthquakes. A material called magnetorheological fluid, or MR fluid, is being used to keep buildings steadier during earthquakes. MR fluid can turn into a solid in the presence of a magnetic force. Once the force is removed, the substance becomes liquid again.

To help reduce earthquake damage in buildings, MR fluid is placed in containers called dampers. Dampers sit on the floor of a building. They are attached to braces and beams. If sensors detect an earthquake, electric magnets are turned on.

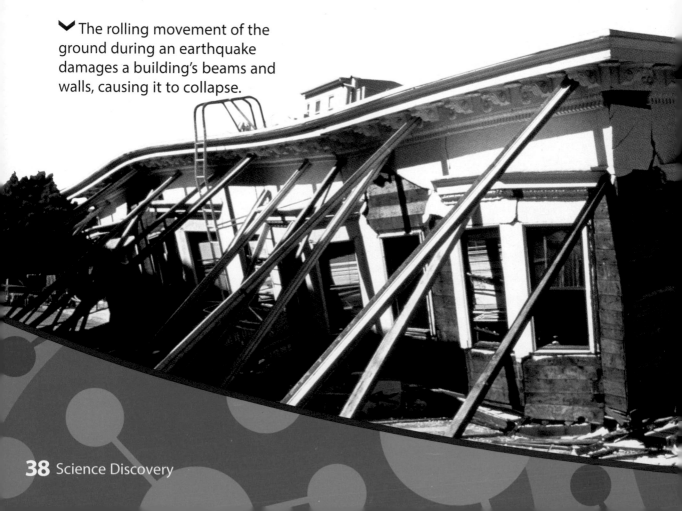

❯ The rolling movement of the ground during an earthquake damages a building's beams and walls, causing it to collapse.

This causes the MR fluid in the dampers to stiffen. This allows the building to sway with the vibrations, minimizing the shock. In the case of severe earthquakes, the MR fluid inside the dampers becomes solid. MR fluid helps the dampers apply more force to stabilize the building. This prevents major damage to the structure of the building.

This technology saves lives by preventing buildings from collapsing during earthquakes. MR fluid is also used in other structures, such as bridges.

Digging Deeper

Your Challenge!

Research past earthquakes and how they impacted different structures. Collect pictures of structures that were damaged in the earthquake and those that were not. How are the structures different?

Summary

It is important to build safe structures. Magnetorheological fluid, or MR fluid, is sometimes used to help keep structures safe during earthquakes.

Further Inquiry

People rely on buildings to keep them safe, but they also rely on other structures, such as bridges. Maybe we should ask,

How are bridges built?

How Are Bridges Built?

Anyone can build a basic bridge. One example is a plank of wood placed across a stream that allows someone to cross without getting wet. However, bridges that support thousands of cars or people are much more complicated to build.

As bridges span greater distances, the **forces** acting on them increase. Compression and tension are two forces that bridge engineers face. Compression is the force of pushing down on an object. Tension occurs when an object is pulled on both ends, such as when a rope is pulled during a game of tug-of-war. On a bridge, too much compression can cause the surface to bend, and too much tension can cause it to snap.

❯ Bridge construction usually begins at each end of the bridge and works towards the middle.

To avoid these problems, bridge designers spread the pressure over a large area. For example, the long, solid beam of a beam bridge spreads out the pressure to the ends, each of which is supported by a column.

The beam bridge is the most common type of bridge. Other bridge types include truss, arch, cantilever, suspension, and cable-stay. Each type is designed to carry loads differently.

Steel or concrete beams are added to bridge designs to support the weight of the structure. Designers often add a lattice to the beams. A lattice is a system of triangles placed together to make the bridge more rigid. It further absorbs the forces of compression and tension.

Digging Deeper

Your Challenge!

Discover how Popsicle stick bridges are built by searching the Internet for Popsicle bridge videos. Some of the videos even test the bridges to see how much weight they can hold. Then try to build your own.

Summary

Compression and tension are important factors engineers must consider when designing a bridge. Too much compression can cause the surface of a bridge to buckle, and excess tension can cause it to snap. Engineers have come up with solutions to both problems.

Further Inquiry

Understanding construction involves asking many questions. Maybe we are ready to put it all together and answer the question, Maybe we should ask,

How are buildings constructed?

Putting It all Together

People live and work in a variety of structures. Sometimes, old buildings are demolished to make way for new ones. The size and shape of a new structure depends on its purpose. Whatever the structure, it takes a great deal of planning to build it. Engineers and architects must consider many details when designing a building. They might borrow styles from other buildings or create something entirely new and innovative.

Before a building's construction can begin, the land must be prepared. Different types of tools and machines are used to build structures. Specialized equipment and machines that help build structures include bulldozers, cranes, and excavators.

It is important that buildings are safe for people to use and enjoy. Skyscrapers are very tall buildings. To ensure the safety of the people who live and work in them, they must be designed to withstand the forces of nature. Elevators help people in skyscrapers move quickly from floor to floor. People also use structures such as bridges to move from place to place.

Where People Fit In

Engineers, architects, contractors, and other construction workers dedicate much time and energy into designing, planning, and building structures. From the time of the pyramids of Egypt to today's skyscrapers, these workers have been creating better ways to build. New methods of construction will continue to make buildings stronger, safer, and easier to use.

⌄ Only 20 percent of people lived in cities 100 years ago. Today, more than half of the world's population is concentrated in cities.

Careers in Construction

Structural Engineer

Structural engineers are often on site throughout the building process. It is their job to identify the best way to build a structure so that it will support its own weight and withstand outside forces. These engineers have a role in building a variety of structures, such as homes, sports stadiums, and oil rigs.

Structural engineers use math and physics to understand how parts of a building will affect each other. They must be familiar with different building materials. This way, they can choose the appropriate materials for the job. The construction process must follow the structural engineer's instructions at every step.

Architect

Architects design structures. They determine what is built on a construction site. Architects must go to a university. Here, they learn how to design safe, useful, and appealing structures.

To begin, architects work with clients to develop ideas about what kind of structure to create. They take these ideas and create plans and models to show clients what the design will look like once it is finished. After the plans are approved, architects work closely with engineers and construction contractors to make sure all of the requirements are met and the local building codes are followed.

Young Scientists at Work

Building can be fun. Use the principles of bridge design discussed in this book to build a small, sturdy bridge.

Materials:

toothpicks

marshmallows

Popsicle sticks

glue

Instructions:

1. Poke a toothpick halfway through the sides of two marshmallows. Then, poke another toothpick halfway through the top of each marshmallow.

2. Poke the other ends of the toothpicks into another marshmallow. This forms a triangle with a marshmallow at each point.

3. Continue connecting toothpicks and marshmallows until you have three triangles. These will make up one side of the bridge.

4. Repeat this process to build the other side of the bridge.

5. Place one side flat on the table. Then, place toothpicks through each corner of the triangles.

6. Connect the other side of the bridge to these toothpicks. This completes the frame of the bridge.

7. To build the roadway, glue Popsicle sticks to the bottom section of the bridge. Test the strength of the bridge with everyday item, such as a toy car.

Observations:

How well did your marshmallow bridge hold up?

How much weight did the bridge hold?

How could you improve your bridge design?

Quiz

Choose a structure you are familiar with to answer more questions. You can choose the place you live, your school buildings, or any other structure. Answer these questions.

Are there blueprints for this structure? Where might the plans be found?

Are any parts of the structure's architecture similar to other buildings in the area?

About how many people use this building each day?

How might this structure be improved?

What materials were used to construct this structure?

Who built this structure?

How old is this building?

Key Words

architect: a person who designs buildings

contractors: people who do a certain job for an agreed price on a construction site

demolition: the act of tearing down or destroying something

engineer: a person who uses science and math to design and build things

forces: a push or pull that causes an object to move

pharaoh: an ancient Egyptian ruler

plantation: a large farm

simple machine: a machine with no moving parts that makes work easier by changing the amount of force needed to do a job

three-dimensional: describes a picture that shows the depth of objects and distances

virtual tour: a tour of a building using a smart phone or computer instead of visiting the building

Index

Log on to www.av2books.com

AV² by Weigl brings you media enhanced books that support active learning. Go to www.av2books.com, and enter the special code found on page 2 of this book. You will gain access to enriched and enhanced content that supplements and complements this book. Content includes video, audio, weblinks, quizzes, a slide show, and activities.

AV² Online Navigation

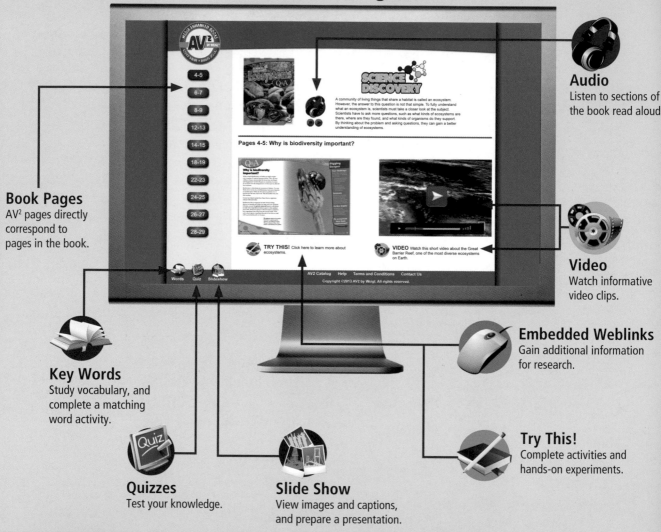

Audio
Listen to sections of the book read aloud.

Book Pages
AV² pages directly correspond to pages in the book.

Video
Watch informative video clips.

Key Words
Study vocabulary, and complete a matching word activity.

Embedded Weblinks
Gain additional information for research.

Quizzes
Test your knowledge.

Slide Show
View images and captions, and prepare a presentation.

Try This!
Complete activities and hands-on experiments.

AV² was built to bridge the gap between print and digital. We encourage you to tell us what you like and what you want to see in the future.

Sign up to be an AV² Ambassador at www.av2books.com/ambassador.